# "HERE COMES BOBBY ORR"

by Robert B. Jackson

*illustrated with photographs*

Henry Z. Walck, Inc.     New York

## U. S. 1930698

The photographs on pages 10, 19, 22, 26, 28, 35, 38, 41, 42, 46, 48, 50, 53, 56, 58, 61 and 63 were supplied by United Press International. Those on pages 14 and 33 are from Wide World Photos, Inc.

# CONTENTS

1. *Goal!*,  9

2. *An Early Start*,  11

3. *The Oshawa Generals*,  17

4. *Bobby Becomes a Bruin*,  24

5. *Boston Superstar*,  30

6. *Stanley Cup Season*,  39

7. *"Les Canadiens Sont Là,"*  49

8. *"Here Comes Bobby Orr,"*  60

# 1

## *GOAL !*

As the slap shot came whistling at Bobby Orr, the young blond Bruin defenseman dropped quickly to one knee and blocked it with his chest like a goalie. Back on his skates and smoothly stickhandling almost from the instant the puck dropped before him, he rushed toward center-ice.

Darting around an intended check, the flying Number Four swept a perfect lead pass to the stick of his advancing left wing, then began skating even faster. The pass came streaking back; and Bobby charged across the opposition's blue line, swiftly shuttling the puck before him with a stick that characteristically had only a few twists of tape around the center of its blade.

VOTED BEST DEFENSEMAN IN THE NHL FOUR YEARS IN A ROW, BOBBY IS ALSO A DAZZLING STICKHANDLER.

Keeping his body between the rapidly sliding puck and the oncoming defenseman, Bobby skillfully cut around him to drive on the net at top speed. When he veered and faked shooting to the right, the goalie had to commit himself in that direction; and Bobby fired a lightning-fast wrist shot past the goalie's left shoulder into the upper corner of the net. The red light flashed, Bobby brandished his stick in accomplishment, and hockey's highest-scoring defenseman had still another goal.

*10*

# 2

## *AN EARLY START*

BOBBY (ROBERT GORDON) ORR was born March 20, 1948, in Parry Sound, Ontario, a small tourist town of about six thousand people on Lake Huron, one hundred and twenty-five miles north of Toronto. His father, Doug Orr, loaded crates at an explosives plant there; and his mother, Arva, worked as a waitress in a local motel to help support a family of two girls and three boys, Bobby being the middle child.

Bobby's grandfather, Robert Orr, who came to Canada from Ireland, had once been a professional soccer player; and Bobby's father was an excellent winger when he played junior hockey as a boy in Canada. Doug was so good, in fact, that at the age of seventeen he was offered a tryout with a Boston Bruin farm team in the Eastern Hockey League.

This was just at the beginning of World War II, however, and Doug decided to enlist in the Navy instead. By the time the war was over he had married and was starting to raise a family. These added responsibilities as well as his age meant the chance to begin a career as a professional athlete was gone; and he settled down to a quiet life in Parry Sound with his wife and children.

The winter that Bobby was four years old, Doug started teaching him how to skate on their frozen backyard. Bobby needed a hockey stick to hold himself up at first; but he soon demonstrated great natural ability and improved rapidly with regular practice. Supervised by his father on the days that Doug worked the night shift, Bobby quickly developed into an excellent skater, the basic requirement for any aspiring hockey player.

As he grew older Bobby naturally progressed to hockey itself, played everywhere and at every age level throughout the long, cold winters in Canada. He began on a neighborhood rink that his father had built on the Seguin River near their home, and then moved out to the Sound for pickup games that involved all the young players of Parry Sound at the same time. Among the boys he played with there were several young Indians from Parry Island who used tree branches as hockey sticks.

When there were no games and during the summer, Bobby spent most of his time practicing his shooting. Hour after hour he slammed his left-handed shots against a sheet of tin that his father had mounted on the garage wall, steadily increasing his accuracy and speed.

At the age of five Bobby was more than ready for the highly organized system of Canadian amateur hockey; and he started out in the local Minor Squirt League. He moved up to Squirt hockey when he was six, and could carry the puck through an entire team by the time he was nine, according to his father.

Bobby skipped the Peewee level entirely to enter Bantam competition when he was twelve. His Parry Sound Bantam team was a strong contender for the Ontario championship in 1960; and he was probably highly disappointed when they lost the final game of the playoffs, 1-0. Far more important in the long run, however, was the fact that several Boston Bruin executives happened to be scouting an earlier contest in the series.

They had originally come to see two players on the opposing team; but Bobby's performance as a defenseman immediately caught their eye. In spite of being younger and smaller than the other Bantams, he easily won the Most Valuable Player award for the tournament; and the Bruin scouts were amazed at how the blond twelve-year-old in a baggy uniform could already stickhandle and shoot like a big-leaguer.

At the time Bobby was only five feet, two inches tall; and he weighed one hundred and ten pounds at the most. It would also be six years before he could even begin to play professional hockey; nevertheless the Bruins were so impressed they decided to try signing him as soon as possible.

AUTOGRAPH SEEKERS CROWD AROUND BOBBY DURING A RETURN VISIT TO HIS HOME TOWN OF PARRY SOUND, ONTARIO.

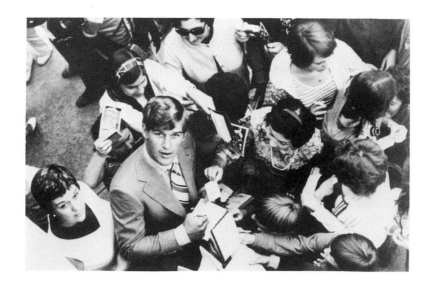

Boston's first move was to give one thousand dollars a year in support of the Parry Sound amateur hockey program. The Bruin officials next started besieging the Orr family with recruiting visits, all the while trying to keep Bobby's ability a secret from the rest of the National Hockey League.

The other clubs found out, anyway, of course; and soon the Montreal Canadiens, the Chicago Black Hawks, the Toronto Maple Leafs and the Detroit Red Wings were also telephoning and sending representatives to plead with the Orrs. One team even approached Bobby's high school principal; but during all this maneuvering the Bruins managed to keep an inside track with Bobby's parents.

When Bobby was fourteen he attended a Bruin try-out camp for amateurs at Niagara Falls, Ontario, during his summer vacation. Although the other boys at the camp were much older, Bobby turned out to be the most skilled played there by far; and Boston intensified its campaign to secure him shortly afterwards.

The final negotiations took place around the Orr kitchen table during the Labor Day weekend of 1962. It has been reported that part of the agreement reached there was for Boston to stucco the Orrs' house, buy a secondhand car for Bobby's father, and get Bobby a new set of clothes. Whatever the actual arrangements were, Bobby signed to play amateur Junior A hockey with the Oshawa, Ontario, Generals, a Bruin-sponsored team in the Ontario Hockey Association. And since National Hockey League rules then in effect specified that when eighth-grader Bobby agreed to play amateur hockey for Oshawa he also committed himself to Boston for his entire big-league career, the Bruins had made one of the shrewdest bargains in the history of professional sport.

## 3

## *THE OSHAWA GENERALS*

THE ORR FAMILY is a very close one; and at the time
Bobby signed to play for Oshawa his mother insisted
that he continue living at home. The Bruins agreed;
and during Bobby's first season in the Ontario Hockey
Association his father drove him back and forth to
Oshawa for each game, a three-hundred-mile round
trip.

Living so far away, Bobby had few chances to practice with the Generals. The other players in the league
were also older and far more experienced than he was,
some of them only one year away from playing professional hockey. In spite of these disadvantages, four-
teen-year-old Bobby not only held his own against the

tough competition, he proved so good he was named to the All-Star second team at the end of the season.

During Bobby's second year with the Generals, his parents allowed him to transfer to a high school in Oshawa and board with a family there. (The Bruins, who paid his tuition and board bills, also gave him spending money each week.) No longer a rookie, and able to practice regularly, Bobby improved to the point of becoming a unanimous choice as an All-Star defenseman. Equally effective on offense, he scored twenty-nine goals over the season, including one three-goal hat trick.

Bobby's twenty-nine goals in 1963-64 broke the previous OHA record of twenty for a defenseman, set by Jacques Laperriere when he was with the Montreal Junior Canadiens. Laperriere had been nineteen years old when he established the mark, however; and Bobby was only fifteen when he broke it. Bobby also had forty-three assists that year, giving him a total of seventy-two points.

He set another scoring record his third season by increasing his goal production to thirty-four; and during 1964-65 he also made fifty-nine assists to accumulate ninety-three points. Since these would have been impressive statistics for a star forward, they represented a very much greater accomplishment for a de-

BOBBY SCORES AN UNASSISTED GOAL AGAINST THE MONTREAL
CANADIENS IN 1970. NUMBER TWO IS JACQUES LAPERRIERE, THE
DEFENSEMAN WHOSE OHA SCORING RECORD BOBBY BROKE WHEN
HE WAS ONLY FIFTEEN.

fenseman who was also one of the best at his primary
responsibility of preventing goals. Sportswriters therefore took to comparing Bobby to a pitcher who could
win both twenty games and a batting championship in
the same year; and he became so well known that his
picture appeared on the cover of a national magazine
in Canada.

About the only thing that hockey experts could find
wrong with Bobby at the time was his size. At sixteen

he was five feet, nine inches tall and he weighed one hundred and sixty-six pounds, relatively small for Junior hockey. But then as now his exceptional skill and mobility more than made up for his lack of height and weight on offense; and he could check as hard as anyone.

As a teen-ager Bobby was even more occupied with hockey than in his younger years. Among the few exceptions were high school, where he studied refrigeration, and his summer vacations. During the off-season he worked at such jobs in Parry Sound as helping a school janitor, being a stock boy in a men's clothing store, and clerking in his uncle's butcher shop. He also went fishing, his favorite activity next to hockey, as often as he could. In addition he followed an extensive year-round exercise program to make himself stronger and heavier; but otherwise most of his time was spent on the ice.

During his fourth and most successful season with Oshawa, Bobby scored thirty-eight goals and made fifty-six assists for ninety-four points. Under his leadership as captain the Generals won the OHA Junior A championship for 1965-66, went on to take the Eastern Canadian championship, and then met the Edmonton Oil Kings for the Junior championship of Canada.

The sixth game of the finals with Edmonton was

critical for the Generals because they were down three games to two. Making matters worse, Bobby had recently suffered a groin injury; and there was considerable controversy over whether he should play or not. The Bruins were concerned that he might injure himself further; but in spite of their objections and the great pain involved, Bobby could not be stopped from competing. His ordeal was all in vain, however; for Edmonton was able to defeat Oshawa and win the championship in what proved to be Bobby's last game as an amateur.

Bobby became eighteen on March 20, 1966—a day the Bruins had been awaiting for six long years. Any NHL team would have been more than happy to have NHL become eligible to join their organization, of course; but the Bruins had to be especially pleased because they were among hockey's biggest losers at the time.

Season after season the Boston club had been playing some of the dreariest hockey in the league. They had finished in last place five of the past seven years and next-to-last the other two. They had also failed to place a player on the All-Star team for thirteen years; and they had not won a league championship since seven years before Bobby was born.

Even Bobby called the Bruins of that period "just

BOBBY, AT THE BEGINNING OF HIS NHL CAREER, HAD NOT YET BEEN
ASSIGNED HIS FAMILIAR NUMBER FOUR.

the worst team going." He later explained that he had
signed with them because he thought he would get
more ice-time as a rookie in Boston than playing for a
better team. The Bruins and their fans had far more

confidence in Bobby's ability than he did, however; and they were counting on him to turn the weak and stumbling team into a big winner all by himself.

While the excitement about Bobby's coming was growing daily in Boston during the summer of 1966, he and the Bruins were conducting lengthy salary negotiations in Canada. Bobby and his father eventually decided to be represented by a young Toronto lawyer, R. Alan Eagleson; and at one point the bargaining was interrupted by the Bruins because they thought Eagleson was asking for too much money. When the lawyer then suggested Bobby might play for the Canadian national amateur team instead, the Boston management changed its mind and came to terms.

The final agreement was signed on board a cabin cruiser anchored near Parry Sound; and the total amount has usually been estimated to be approximately $75,000 over a two-year period. Before this contract hockey players had been among the poorest paid of professional athletes; and even Bobby's salary was not large when compared to those of superstars in other sports. Nevertheless, as the highest amount ever paid an NHL rookie it was a major advance for hockey player; and as a result their salaries have been rising rapidly ever since.

# 4

## *BOBBY BECOMES A BRUIN*

AT THE TIME BOBBY became the highest-paid and most publicized rookie in the history of the National Hockey League, he was still a shy and very quiet youngster. His skills on the ice were already of unquestioned big-league quality; but there was still much for him to learn about people and life outside Parry Sound.

When he first reported to the Bruins he was something of a loner, bashfully calling the other players "Sir" and "Mister." "I was like a kid in a new school," Bobby later told an interviewer, "I was afraid to talk or anything."

And while everyone else was certain that Bobby would eventually develop into an NHL superstar, he himself was unconvinced that he could even stay in the league. "I really didn't think I was going to make it," he has said.

But when his ability and likable personality gained Bobby the quick acceptance of his Bruin teammates, he began to feel more at home in Boston. His poise and self-confidence also gradually increased as he became more familiar with the NHL and came to realize his own competence.

Opposition players did take advantage of Bobby's inexperience in the beginning, however. He has told of a New York game during which he heard a voice behind him shout, "I've got a clear shot, Bobby. Drop it!" Assuming it was a Bruin, Bobby drop passed the puck, only to discover the voice belonged to a Ranger who promptly scored.

NHL hockey being a rough, violent and often brutal game, Bobby's courage was also put to the test early in his professional career. Longtime superstar Gordie Howe of the Detroit Red Wings has been quoted as saying, "If you find you can push someone around, then you push him around"; and each of the opposing teams had a try at pushing Bobby. They soon learned that while he might be mild-mannered out of uniform, he was not about to let anyone muscle him out of position on the ice.

"I never had a fight in my life until I came to Boston," Bobby once told a reporter; and although this may be a slight exaggeration, it is certainly true that he had a number of battles when he first joined the Bruins. Refusing to back away from the slightest challenge, Bobby soon established his present reputation as a clean but aggressively tough player. "Some people think fighting is terrible," he has commented, "but I think the odd scrap—without sticks—is part of the game." (One Canadian magazine has since listed

BOBBY IS IN THE THICK OF THIS BRUIN-CANADIEN STRUGGLE FOR THE PUCK IN FRONT OF THE BOSTON GOAL EARLY IN HIS ROOKIE SEASON.

him as Number Three on their list of the ten best fighters in the NHL.)

Bobby's first regular appearance in the National Hockey League was against the Detroit Red Wings; and he recalls being so excited about making his professional debut that he arrived at four-thirty in the afternoon to get ready for an eight P.M. game. The Bruins beat the Wings, with Bobby getting his first NHL point for an assist on a goal by Johnny Bucyk. Bobby has since admitted that what appeared to be a clever pass to Bucyk for the assist was really only an attempted shot on which he partially fanned.

He was successful in scoring his first big-league goal in only his third game, however; and it came against the champion Montreal Canadiens—a blazing, forty-five-foot slap shot that goalie Gump Worsley never even saw. Afterwards Doug Orr, who was at Boston Garden that night, proudly had the puck gold-plated.

Young Bobby had already become a favorite of the always demonstrative Bruin fans; and when he scored that first goal the Garden spectators stood to cheer and applaud for a full three minutes. His sparkling play also made many new followers for the Bruins as the season progressed; and total attendance at Boston Garden during 1966-67 increased by many thousand because of his addition to the team.

The hockey experts were just as excited by Bobby's play as his fans, marveling at his ability to score goals as well as avert them. Emile Francis, General Manager and Coach of the New York Rangers, has commented, "Nobody else can do the things that Orr can do. If they tried, they'd make fools of themselves." Bill Chadwick, well-known former referee and member of the Hockey Hall of Fame, once said, "Imagining a better hockey player is beyond my comprehension." And NHL president Clarence Campbell told a news maga-

AN OVERWHELMING CHOICE FOR ROOKIE OF THE YEAR IN 1966–67, BOBBY DEMONSTRATES HIS DEFT PUCK CONTROL BEHIND THE TORONTO MAPLE LEAF NET.

zine, "I've seen all the greats since the 1920's, and I've never seen a player with the skills of Orr."

During the sixty-one games that Bobby played in his first year with the Bruins he scored thirteen goals and had twenty-eight assists for a total of forty-one points. At the conclusion of the season he was named to the All-Star second team and received 168 of a possible 180 points in the voting for the Calder Memorial Trophy, awarded to the NHL rookie of the year. Veteran Harry Howell of New York received the James Norris Memorial Trophy for being the outstanding defenseman of 1966-67; but afterwards he was quoted as saying, "I'm glad I won it now. No one else but Orr will win it for the next twenty years."

# 5

## *BOSTON SUPERSTAR*

BOBBY HAD EITHER SCORED or assisted on nearly one-fourth of Boston's goals during 1966-67, remarkable for any defenseman, much less a rookie. But not even this brilliant performance was enough to save the Bruins from still another last-place finish in Bobby's first year with the team.

That spring Milt Schmidt, a former Bruin captain and coach, took over as General Manager of the club; and one of his first decisions was to arrange a trade bringing Phil Esposito, Fred Stanford and Ken Hodge to Boston from the Chicago Black Hawks. He also moved Harry Sinden up from Oklahoma City as coach. These changes in combination with Bobby's growing experience plus the improved morale that resulted from the reorganization would eventually make the difference for the Bruins; but there were to be further difficulties immediately ahead.

During August of 1967 Bobby tore ligaments in his right knee while playing in a benefit game and had to spend five weeks wearing a cast. Then, early in November, the controversial Conacher fight occurred. The Bruins were playing the Toronto Maple Leafs in Boston Garden when Leaf wing Brian Conacher collided with Bobby. Bobby's nose was broken, many think accidentally; but he was apparently convinced that Conacher had high-sticked him intentionally, and he gave chase.

When he caught up with Conacher, Bobby punched him furiously until he was dragged away. Afterwards he was quoted as saying, "A guy can beat me with his fists and I won't complain, but not with the stick. I hate sticks." Even the usually loyal Boston press commented on the way Bobby lost his temper; and one reporter pointed out that, if nothing else, Bobby hurt the Bruins by being in the penalty box afterwards instead of on the ice. The same reporter also emphasized the possibility of needless injury occurring during such fights.

And, as Bobby was shortly to discover, it was injuries

that were going to threaten his otherwise excellent chance of becoming hockey's greatest star. About a month later, while taking a hard body check, he broke his collarbone and also suffered a shoulder separation. Even worse, not long after he had recovered from these injuries, he hurt his left knee. An operation was necessary, forcing him out of action for the latter part of the season.

Bobby's absences from the lineup were particularly critical to the 1967-68 Bruins because by then the team had improved to the point of becoming a championship contender. Impossible as it must have seemed to many a long-suffering Bruin fan, the revitalized club actually occupied first place of the Eastern Division early in the season and was fighting the New York Rangers for second near its end.

Although Bobby did manage to play in the last few games of the regular season, he had not yet fully recovered—a major reason why Boston slipped to a third-place finish behind Montreal and New York in the East. But since the first four finishers in each of the two NHL divisions during the regular season engage in a lengthy series of playoffs to determine the league champion and winner of the famous Stanley Cup, the Bruins then went on to make their first playoff appearance in nine years.

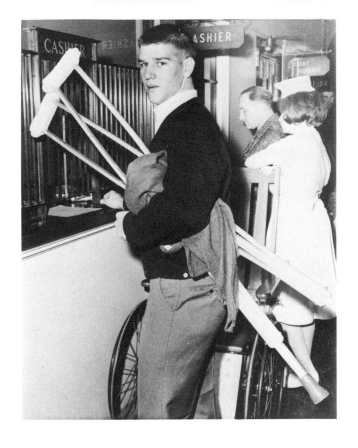

INJURIES HAVE SERIOUSLY THREATENED BOBBY'S CAREER FROM
TIME TO TIME. HERE HE CHECKS OUT OF A HOSPITAL AFTER TREAT-
MENT FOR STRAINED KNEE LIGAMENTS IN 1966.

With Bobby still not up to par, it was a brief and
generally ineffectual performance, however. The fast-
skating Montreal Canadiens eliminated Boston by defeating them in four straight games, beat Chicago to
take the Eastern Division, and then overwhelmed St.
Louis of the West to win the Stanley Cup for a record

fourteenth time since the National Hockey League was founded. In contrast Boston had not won a Stanley Cup since 1941.

Of the seventy-four games on the Bruins' regular schedule during 1967-68, Bobby had been able to play in only forty-six because of his injuries. Nevertheless, he accumulated thirty-one points, eleven goals and twenty assists, and was selected for the All-Star team. He also received the James Norris Memorial trophy for being the best defenseman in the NHL after only his second year in the league.

But by spring Bobby's future as a hockey player was in some doubt. He had returned to the ice too soon after his knee operation in February; and the pain was now extreme. Three days after Parry Sound's big "Bobby Orr Day" celebration in June, he had to go back into the hospital for further cartilage removal.

While Bobby was recuperating during the summer of 1968, lawyer Eagleson negotiated a new, three-year contract for him with the Bruins. The total amount was often said to be $400,000, but was more likely to have been closer to $200,000. Still, it was a very large amount (particularly for a player who was gaining a reputation for being brittle) ; and it touched off increased salary demands all around the league.

When the Boston training camp opened in September, Bobby could barely skate; and he did not play in any of the Bruin exhibition games. Unable even to practice until one week before the season began, he then came back so quickly that he took his regular turns in the opener against Detroit and followed Coach Sinden's usual practice of having him kill penalties and work the power plays as well. On the ice for a total of twenty-five minutes, he not only took some hard shots to his left knee without incident, he also scored on one of his patented net-to-net stick-handling displays. **U. S. 1930698**

Apparently in top playing condition again and get-

BOBBY TAKES THE PUCK AWAY FROM A ST. LOUIS BLUES WINGER WHO HAD BEEN DRIVING ON THE BOSTON GOAL, NOVEMBER, 1968.

ting off to a fine start on his third NHL season, Bobby scored a hat trick against the Chicago Black Hawks on the night of December 16, 1968. His first goal came on a power play; he rushed three-quarters the length of the rink to score his second; and the third was a slap shot from the blue line that caused the crowd in Boston Garden to explode. They shouted, cheered, and applauded loudly, scaling dozens of hats onto the ice to salute his accomplishment and holding up the game for some time. (Bobby's typically understated comment afterwards was, "Too bad I've never worn a hat.")

Then suddenly in late January Bobby reinjured his knee and could not play again until the end of February, a heavy blow to Boston's 1969 championship hopes. Before he left the lineup Boston had been completely dominating the East; by the time he got back the Bruins had lost their edge and were battling the Montreal Canadiens for the divisional lead. During a bitter struggle over the second half of the season the two teams swapped first place eight times, Montreal finally clinched the top spot by defeating Boston in the next-to-last game of the regular schedule.

Both Boston and Montreal next won their first-round playoffs, which meant they continued their rivalry by playing each other for the Eastern Championship. These semifinals were particularly important in 1969 because the Western Division of the NHL, which started playing in 1967, was then composed entirely of expansion clubs. The club winning in the East was thus virtually certain of taking the overall championship in the East-West finals, none of the expansion clubs being nearly as good as the original NHL members.

Boston made a promising start in the exciting series, leading each of the first two games until the final ninety seconds. But in both cases the Bruins made mistakes allowing Montreal to tie; and the Canadiens went on to win in overtime twice. Undaunted, Boston came back to win the third and fourth games to even the series, the fourth game going to the Bruins on the strength of Bobby's third-period goal.

Montreal next won the fifth meeting, putting the Bruins' backs to the wall in the sixth. Facing elimination, Boston again scored early, and once more led going into the third period; but once again the Canadiens were able to tie. The two teams then fought evenly throughout the first overtime period and most of the second—until Canadien captain Jean Beliveau scored from directly in front of the net to give Montreal the game, a victory in the East, and, ultimately, the Stanley Cup as well.

THE BRUINS BEAT THE CANADIENS, 3-2, IN THEIR FOURTH PLAYOFF GAME OF 1969 ON THE STRENGTH OF THIS THIRD-PERIOD GOAL BY BOBBY. THE PUCK IS JUST ENTERING THE NET BEHIND THE MONTREAL GOALIE.

But if his team was to need still another season to reach its peak, Bobby did not. During 1968-69 he scored twenty-one goals and made forty-three assists for sixty-four points, breaking the previous records for both points and goals scored by an NHL defenseman. He also received the highest number of votes for the All-Star team; and was awarded the Norris trophy as the outstanding defenseman in the league for the second year in a row.

# 6

## *STANLEY CUP SEASON*

ALTHOUGH NEARLY EVERYONE anticipated a big year for the Bruins in 1969-70, the beginning of their season was hardly promising. Training camp had barely started when right wing Ken Hodge had to have his appendix removed; and several other Bruins then received disabling injuries in the course of training itself.

Next came a shameful stick-swinging fight between Boston's Ted Green and Wayne Maki of the St. Louis Blues during an exhibition game. Green, known as one of hockey's roughest defensemen and sometimes called "The Enforcer," had his skull fractured, making two brain operations necessary and putting him out of action for the entire season.

Serious injuries continued to trouble the Bruins when defenseman Rick Smith cracked a rib in the opening game of the regular schedule, and mod center Derek Sanderson crashed into a goal post in the second contest after being tripped. The popular Sanderson reinjured a knee in his accident, was hospitalized, and could not play for five weeks.

There was one notable absence from the Bruins' injury list, however, and it was Bobby. He did cut his lower lip several times at the start of the season, requiring a total of twenty-eight stitches; but in his terms this was only "Band-Aid stuff." The important thing was that his previously troublesome knees held up perfectly all season long.

In a sense Bobby's knees carried all of the Bruins, for he was publicly acknowledged by several of his teammates to have become the leader of the club by then. Although Bobby was only twenty-one years old at the time, he had matured greatly in his three preceding seasons with Boston and had come a long way indeed from the early days when he called the other players "Sir."

Hockey experts had predicted that Boston would challenge the long-established dominance of the Montreal Canadiens during 1969-70; and the Bruins lived up to this forecast in spite of their many injuries. Not as expected, however, was the fact that the New York Rangers proved strong enough to battle the Bruins for first place throughout much of the season.

New York edged into the lead in the middle of November and then played well enough to hold a paper-slim margin of only a few points over Boston for more than three months. Meanwhile, Bobby became the only unanimous choice for the All-Star game in January and continued to lead the NHL in scoring throughout the period, the first defenseman to do so for more than just a few games at the beginning of a season.

BOBBY WAS THE ONLY UNANIMOUS CHOICE FOR THE NHL ALL-STAR GAME IN JANUARY OF 1970.

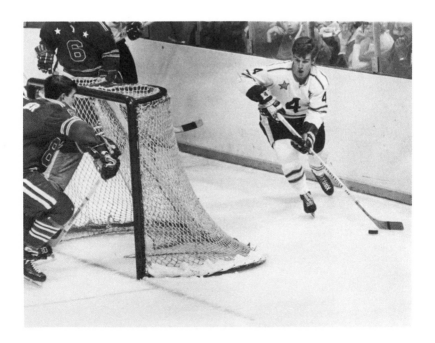

But on March first the Rangers dropped from first place, beginning a late-season slump that eventually caused them to finish fourth and barely make the play-offs. When New York faltered, the Bruins immediately took over the lead in the East, only to find themselves pursued before long by the surging Chicago Black Hawks; and this Boston-Chicago struggle went right down to the last day of the season.

In one of the closest finishes ever seen in the NHL, the Bruins and Hawks remained tied for first place in the East, even after the last game of the schedule had been played. League positions are ordinarily determined on a points basis (two for a win, one for a tie) ;

TWO-THIRDS OF THE MONTREAL TEAM UNSUCCESSFULLY CONCEN-
TRATES ON BOBBY DURING THE FINAL REGULAR GAME OF THE
1970–71 SEASON.

but to settle the ninety-nine-point Bruin-Hawk dead-lock, the total number of victories for each team had to be considered under an old rule. This procedure gave first place to Chicago (forty-five wins as compared to Boston's forty) ; and was not a very popular one in Boston, of course, particularly since the Hawks had lost five more games than the Bruins.

The Detroit Red Wings finished a clean third in the East for 1969-70, four points out of first. Fourth position was even more closely contested than first, however, New York and Montreal concluding the season with identical won-lost-tied records, only seven points behind Chicago and Boston. When the Rangers were awarded fourth place because of scoring two more goals than the Canadiens over the seventy-six games, it meant that Montreal had failed to make the playoffs for the first time in twenty-two years. Even more unusual, since the Toronto Maple Leafs finished sixth in the East, no Canadian-based team was represented in Stanley Cup competition in 1970 for the first time in history.

Although the contending teams were very close to each other all season long, no other player even approached Bobby's statistics as he broke record after record. Playing in every game on the regular schedule (which stopped talk of his being injury-prone) , Bobby became the first defenseman to win the NHL scoring title in the fifty-three years the league has existed. His thirty-three goals, eighty-seven assists and one hundred and twenty points were all records for a defenseman; and his eighty-seven assists was an overall record.

Second to Bobby in NHL scoring during 1969-70 was Bruin center Phil Esposito with ninety-nine points, the highest total for a single season in the NHL; and the Bruins therefore entered the Stanley Cup playoffs in 1970 with the two best scorers in the league.

As the second-place finisher in the East, Boston's first opponent was fourth-place New York; and in the opener the Bruins trampled the Rangers, 8-2, with Bobby getting two goals and Phil three. Boston took the second game as well, 5-3; then dropped the third and fourth, 4-3 and 4-2, in spite of the fact that Bobby and Phil raised their series totals to four goals each. Boston came back to win the critical fifth game, 3-2, however, as both Bobby and Phil scored again; and the Bruins eliminated New York in the sixth encounter, 4-1, with Bobby making his sixth and seventh goals of the series.

"The kid did it all in six games. If we had him, no one ever would touch us. What a player!" Ranger Coach and General Manager Emile Francis commented afterwards. "Without that kid, it's an even series."

Meanwhile first-place Chicago had disposed of third-place Detroit in four straight games, setting the stage for a confrontation between Boston and Chicago in the Eastern Finals. This series received even more attention in the national press than usual because of Chicago's having overtaken Boston for the divisional lead at the very end of the season and also because of the Esposito rivalry. High-scoring Bruin center Phil Esposito, himself once a Black Hawk, had a younger brother, Tony, who was a rookie-of-the-year goalie for the Hawks; and the playoffs pitted the two brothers directly against each other.

At 12:28 in the first period of the first game, Phil became the first Bruin to score on his brother; and from then on Boston was in complete command. The Bruins swept the Hawks in four straight games, 6-3, 4-1, 5-2 and 5-4, with Phil's five goals being the best scoring effort of the series.

Bobby played his usual strong defense against Chicago, averaging thirty-five minutes a game on the ice. He also scored a goal and made four assists, including a dazzling centering pass in the third game while surrounded by three scrambling Hawks behind the Chicago goal. "He's so good that he can spoil the game

A HAPPY BOBBY RELAXES IN THE DRESSING ROOM AFTER THE
BRUINS TOOK THEIR FOURTH STRAIGHT PLAYOFF GAME FROM THE
CHICAGO BLACK HAWKS IN 1970.

for everybody," Coach Billy Reay of the Black Hawks
later grumbled.

The only obstacle between the Bruins and their first
Stanley Cup in twenty-nine years was now the St.

Louis Blues, winner of the Western Finals and best of the expansion clubs. The Blues had won in the West each year since the division was created; but they had never been able to win a playoff game from the more powerful Eastern teams, and they were certainly overmatched against the Bruins. Boston completely outplayed St. Louis in the series opener, 6-1; trounced them again, 6-2, in the second game; and then took the third easily, 4-1. The East-West playoffs seemed so one-sided at this point that one Boston newspaper called them "Hockey's Answer to Laugh-In."

The fourth game, played in Boston on May 10, 1970, was a different story, however. Boston scored early, only to have St. Louis tie just as the first period was ending. The Blues went ahead, 2-1, in the second period; but Phil Esposito banged in his thirteenth goal of the playoffs to even the score once more. With only seconds gone in the third period, St. Louis next made it 3-2; and until the last few minutes of the game it looked as if this would be the final score. Then, at 13.28 Johnny Bucyk put one in the nets for Boston and sent the game into sudden-death overtime.

The playoffs were suddenly and dramatically ended, however, when Bobby stole the puck from a Blue winger with only half a minute of the overtime gone. He swiftly passed to center Derek Sanderson in the

HAVING JUST MADE THE OVERTIME GOAL THAT FINALLY BROUGHT THE STANLEY CUP TO BOSTON AGAIN, BOBBY TRIPS OVER A STICK AND FALLS TO THE ICE. THE ENTIRE BOSTON TEAM IMMEDIATELY PILED ON TOP OF HIM IN CELEBRATION.

right corner and drove on the goal, taking a return flip from Sanderson just as he reached the net. An instant before he tripped over another player's stick, Bobby acrobatically fired a shot between the St. Louis goalie's legs; and by the time he fell to the ice he had won the game and brought the Stanley Cup back to Boston at last.

# 7

## *"LES CANADIENS SONT LA"*

THE BRUINS HAD an uproarious celebration immediately after winning the Stanley Cup, each of them drinking champagne from the big dented trophy in turn; and later there was a jubilant victory parade through the cramped and winding streets of downtown Boston. Throwing confetti and cheering, thousands of Bruin fans lined the curbs to honor the first championship NHL team in Boston since 1941, twenty-nine years earlier.

Not only were the Bruins finally champions again, they had won their last ten playoff games in a row; and both Phil Esposito and Bobby had established Cup scoring records. Phil made thirteen goals and scored

ELATED BRUIN FANS CROWD BOSTON'S DOWNTOWN STREETS TO
GREET THEIR TEAM AFTER THE STANLEY CUP VICTORY OF 1970.

twenty-seven points for a pair of overall records, while
Bobby broke two previous marks for defensemen with
nine goals and twenty points.

And, of course, Bobby's overtime goal that clinched
the Cup for Boston made him more popular than ever
with Bruin followers. The experts were also highly

impressed by his performance in the playoffs, not to mention all season long; and Bobby swept all the major awards for which he was eligible that season. He won the Conn Smythe Trophy for being the most valuable player of the Cup competition, received the James Norris Memorial Trophy as the best defenseman in the league for the third straight year, and was also awarded the Art Ross Trophy for leading the NHL in scoring. Even greater recognition came when he was named winner of the Hart Memorial Trophy as the most valuable player in the league during 1969-70.

Only four days after the Cup victory, in the midst of all the celebrating, there was surprising news, however. The Bruins announced that Coach Harry Sinden had decided to leave the team because of a salary disagreement. Rookie coach Tom Johnson was then selected to succeed Sinden, a tough assignment for anyone, much less a first-year man.

Even so, Boston was still considered the team to beat when the 1970-71 season opened in mid-October. True to form, the Bruins did not lose a game until the end of the month; but their traditional rivals, the New York Rangers, did equally well. As a result the two clubs were tied for the lead in the East on November first with fifteen points each.

Phil Esposito, off to a fast start in the individual scoring race, led the league at this point with nineteen points in the nine games. Bobby, on the other hand, had injured his wrist in an exhibition game and was scoring at a relatively slow pace for him, thirteenth overall with eleven points.

During November Bobby returned to his usual form and zoomed from thirteenth to second in scoring, totaling thirty-two points. Phil Esposito remained the NHL scoring leader with thirty-nine points at the end of the month, while as a team the Bruins had been able to move only two points in front of the challenging Rangers. Five points behind New York in third place were the once-dominant Montreal Canadiens.

New York persisted in preventing the expected runaway of Boston in the East through the All-Star game in January, approximately the halfway point of the season, scrappily staying within three points of the champions and fifteen points ahead of the Canadiens. Then, during February and March, the Rangers tailed off into another of their customary late-season slumps; and this allowed the Bruins to virtually coast to their first division title and Prince of Wales Trophy in thirty years.

With first place assured in the latter stages of the schedule, the chief source of interest for Boston fans

BOBBY AND TEAMMATE PHIL ESPOSITO AFTER THE MARCH, 1971 GAME IN WHICH BOBBY BROKE THE NHL RECORD FOR GOALS SCORED BY A DEFENSEMAN IN A SEASON, AND PHIL TIED BOBBY HULL'S OVERALL MARK OF FIFTY-EIGHT GOALS IN A YEAR.

became the individual scoring race. The previous high for NHL goals in one season had been Chicago Black Hawk Bobby Hull's fifty-eight; but Phil Esposito demolished that mark by scoring seventy-six. The sad-eyed yet happy-go-lucky Bruin center also made seventy-six assists during 1970-71 to total 152 points, which was another record.

Bobby was runner-up in NHL scoring, his personal

pro high of thirty-seven goals and 139 points being further records for a defenseman, and his 102 assists establishing a new league record. Not only that, Bruins Johnny Bucyk and Ken Hodge were third and fourth in NHL scoring as Boston set a new team mark of 399 goals in one season, 96 goals more than the previous record, also set by Boston. The 1970-71 Bruins smashed thirty-four other league records as well and were thus generally regarded as having the strongest offense ever seen in hockey.

Opposing the Bruin powerhouse in the first round of the 1971 playoffs were the third-place Montreal Canadiens, a team that Boston had defeated five of six times during the regular season, including a 7-2 rout on its final day. The oldest and formerly one of the greatest teams in the NHL, the Canadiens had been slowed in recent years by the advancing age of many of their stars. They had also been troubled by many injuries early in the season as well as coaching difficulties and a marked weakness in goal at times, the overall result being that Montreal finished twenty-four points behind the Bruins.

Still, there is a great pride and strong sense of tradition on the Montreal club and among its fiercely devoted fans, who often sing an old folk song *"Les Canadiens Sont Là"* ("The Canadiens Are There"), to their team on hockey night. After all, Montreal had bested Boston in ten straight playoff series in the past. There was also some talk that the Bruins might have become overconfident after their big season and were perhaps distracted by the many outside business interests their success had brought them. In addition, some people thought the Bruins could have lost much of their momentum when Bobby was rested during the closing games of the regular schedule.

However, the Bruins-Canadien opener took place in dank old Boston Garden where the Bruins had been virtually invincible during the regular season, winning twenty-seven games in a row; and where uninhibited Bruin fans festoon the railings with such banners as "Italian Power!" for Phil Esposito, "Have Orr, Will Score," and "VictORRy Comes NatORRly, of cORRse."

Orr did score the first goal of the big series; but with Boston ahead, 3-1, in the third period he was also penalized two minutes for holding. Feeling that Montreal had gone unpenalized many times for the same offense, he lost his temper over the call and had hot words with the referee, which led to a further ten-minute misconduct penalty. Now completely enraged —a rare state for him—Bobby pushed a linesman aside and started for the referee, stopping only when his

DIVING OVER THE FALLEN BRUIN GOALIE, BOBBY TRIES TO STOP A CANADIEN GOAL IN THE FIRST OF THE BOSTON-MONTREAL 1971 PLAYOFF GAMES.

teammates piled upon him. Although the Bruins were able to maintain their lead without Bobby and he apologized later, everyone was greatly surprised by this unreasonable burst of anger.

Boston's second game in defense of the Stanley Cup was also held in the Garden; and the Bruins broke away to a commanding 5-1 lead, with Bobby scoring one goal and getting three assists. But when Henri

Richard stole the puck away from Bobby in the second period for an unassisted goal, the Bruins seemed to fall apart. Bobby played "the worst thirty minutes of his career" according to one sports magazine as Montreal scored six straight times and came back to stun Boston with a 7-5 defeat at home.

The series next moved to Montreal, where the Canadiens won the third game, 3-1, and were also leading in the fourth, 1-0, at the end of the first period. Back in top form again by now, Bobby golfed one in from the goal line to tie; and Mike Walton put the Bruins ahead, 2-1. Bobby's forty-foot slap shot down the middle in the third period gave Boston a 3-1 edge; and after the score had gone to 4-2 and there were only seconds left, he drove on the goal again. The sensational young Montreal goalie, Ken Dryden, a law student who had been in the nets for the Canadiens only six times at the end of the season before drawing the playoff assignment, had been pulled in favor of a sixth skater; and Bobby cracked the puck into the empty goal. By doing so he not only made the score 5-2, he also completed the only Stanley Cup hat trick scored by a defenseman in forty-four years.

Their morale much improved, the Bruins returned to Boston and beat Montreal once more, 7-3, taking a one-game advantage. At that point they needed only one more victory to retain the Cup; but they were badly outplayed in the critical sixth meeting, 8-3, by the spunky Canadiens; and it all came down to one final meeting in Boston.

One Montreal player had been quoted as saying, "Stop Orr and you stop the Bruins"; and the Canadiens were able to gang up on Bobby and contain him completely during that all-important seventh game. When big rookie goalie Dryden also made several spectacular saves against the other Bruins, Montreal was able to accomplish one of the greatest upsets in Cup history by eliminating Boston from the playoffs, 4-2.

BOBBY KNOCKS A FLYING PUCK TO THE ICE DURING THE SEVENTH GAME OF STANLEY CUP COMPETITION BETWEEN MONTREAL AND BOSTON IN 1971.

The amazing Canadiens were eventually to extend their comeback in 1971 to the point of defeating Chicago in the finals to win the Stanley Cup for a sixteenth time. That was little consolation to the Bruins and their fans, of course, who all summer long had to answer the same old question, "What happened?"

# 8

## *"HERE COMES BOBBY ORR"*

THE ELIMINATION OF THE BRUINS from Stanley Cup competition in seven games had to be a bitter disappointment for Bobby; but when the 1971 awards of the Professional Hockey Writers Association were presented, his outstanding play over the seventy-eight games of the regular season had earned him further honors. He won the James Norris Memorial Trophy as the outstanding NHL defenseman for the fourth consecutive time, a feat that had been accomplished only once before; and he also became the second NHL player to have twice won the Hart Memorial Trophy for being the most valuable player in the league.

Going beyond such annual awards, there is now general agreement that Bobby has become the best

AT THE END OF THE 1970–71 SEASON, BOBBY RECEIVED BOTH THE
JAMES NORRIS MEMORIAL TROPHY AS THE NHL'S OUTSTANDING
DEFENSEMAN AND THE HART MEMORIAL TROPHY FOR BEING THE
LEAGUE'S MOST VALUABLE PLAYER.

defenseman ever to play hockey. Furthermore, many experts also call him the greatest all-around player in the history of the sport. He is the most popular star in the game today as well, both with regular fans and those who would seldom follow hockey otherwise. Even the poorest-drawing NHL teams pack them in when Bobby comes to town; and his quick, dramatic style on the ice has been one of the biggest reasons why interest in hockey has been expanding rapidly in this country.

Bobby is not nearly as dramatic off the ice, being a very likable, quiet and genuinely modest young man who does not seem particularly interested in the fact that he is fast becoming a millionaire. In fact, he has been known to forget to cash large checks for months at a time.

Much of this money is coming from Bobby's many business interests outside the NHL. Besides the usual product endorsements, he runs a summer sports camp for boys with teammate Mike Walton, owns real estate and a restaurant, and controls a growing chain of Bobby Orr's Pizza Places. These activities, which bring Bobby over a quarter million dollars a year, are supervised by Bobby's attorney, R. Alan Eagleson, usually referred to as "The Eagle" by Bobby.

Hockey having taken so much of Bobby's time since

his youth (like the majority of NHL players he did not stay in high school long enough to graduate), he has developed few other interests. He does like to cook —a steak and several eggs before a game, for example; and besides fishing, he swims, water-skis, and plays golf and tennis during the summer. He also devotes much of his time and a great deal of his money to a wide variety of charitable activities, particularly those concerned with children.

Hockey is a very rough game, and Bobby considers it no small accomplishment that he still has his own teeth. But rugged as NHL stars have to be, many

BOBBY TAKES A TURN AROUND THE BOSTON GARDEN ICE WITH TWO DAUGHTERS OF TEAMMATE JOHNNY MCKENZIE. HE HAD RECEIVED THE BLACK EYE IN A GAME TWO DAYS EARLIER.

have played into their forties; and Bobby could possibly have as many as twenty years ahead of him as a professional. During the season of 1970-71, however, Bobby stated that he would play five more years and then "take some time off." He also said that he has no ambition ever to coach hockey; and that when he does retire he will return to Parry Sound because he does not like life in the city.

But judging from the hundreds of bumper stickers reading "This is Orr Country" to be seen all over New England, the ratings when a Bruin game is telecast nationally, and the nearly eighty thousand letters Bobby receives each year, his fans would be decidedly unhappy about an early retirement.

Just as the name of Babe Ruth has become synonymous with baseball and Joe Namath means pro football to nearly everyone, Bobby's name has become the equivalent of his sport. When he finally does leave the ice, hockey will lose its brightest star.